TopReaders

Flight

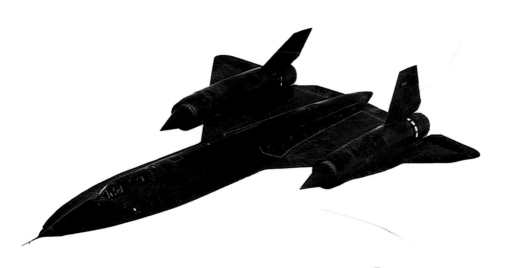

Robert Coupe

Contents

People have always dreamed of being
able to fly. In the last century, airplanes
were developed. For millions of people,
the dream of flying has come true.

Flight in Nature

Animals that fly have wings. When birds fly, they move their wings forward and down, then backward and up. Many insects are also fliers. Bats are flying mammals.

A hummingbird can hover *in one spot. To do this, it moves its wings rapidly in different ways around its body.*

up and down

forward and down

swirling round

high up and round

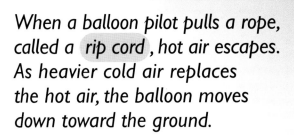

When a balloon pilot pulls a rope, called a rip cord , hot air escapes. As heavier cold air replaces the hot air, the balloon moves down toward the ground.

Hot-air Balloon

People have been flying in balloons for more than 200 years. Burners heat air or gas inside the balloon. It is then lighter than the air outside. The balloon lifts up and is driven by wind currents.

Fact File

In 1783, in Paris, France, two men went up in a balloon designed and built by two brothers named Montgolfier.

Steam Power

During the 1800s, the steam engine was developed. Several people tried to build airplanes powered by steam. Some of these lifted off the ground. None of them flew long distances.

A Model for the Future

In 1842, William Henson built a model airplane. Its steam engine was designed to turn two propellers. It never flew, but it was the first flying invention that really looked like an airplane.

In 1903, Samuel Langley's gasoline -powered airplane was launched from the top of a houseboat on the Potomac River in eastern USA. It plunged straight into the water.

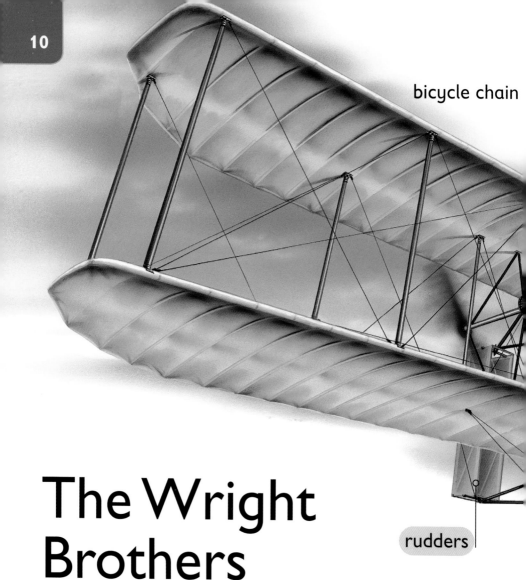

bicycle chain

rudders

The Wright Brothers

Orville and Wilbur Wright developed the first powered airplane. They called it the *Flyer*. In December 1903, Orville made the first flights, in North Carolina, USA. He flew just four times, for a total of 98 seconds.

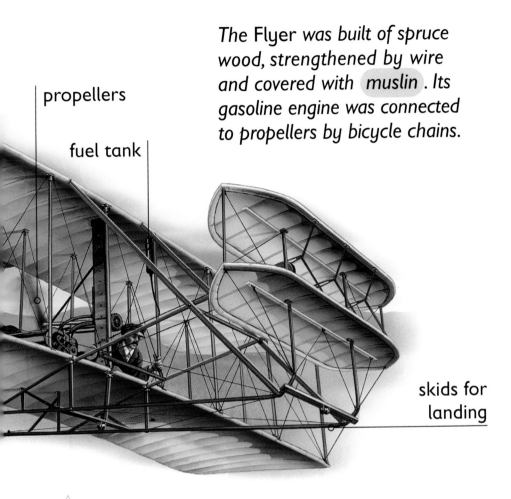

propellers

fuel tank

The Flyer *was built of spruce wood, strengthened by wire and covered with* muslin *. Its gasoline engine was connected to propellers by bicycle chains.*

skids for landing

How Propellers Work

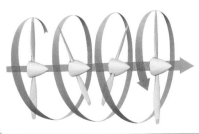

As propellers spin around, they reduce the air pressure in front of them. This pulls the airplane forward. The *Flyer's* propellers were wooden.

Breaking Records

In 1909, Louis Blériot made the first flight from France to England. In 1914, a tiny flying boat in Florida, USA, carried the first passengers. They traveled 21 miles (34 km) in 23 minutes.

Allen had to pedal hard to spin the propeller.

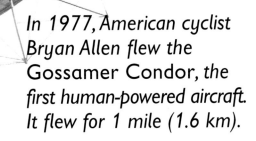

In 1977, American cyclist Bryan Allen flew the Gossamer Condor, the first human-powered aircraft. It flew for 1 mile (1.6 km).

☆Atlantic Crossing

British aviators John Alcock and Arthur Whitten Brown made the first non-stop flight across the Atlantic in 1919 in a Vickers Vimy like this one.

The cockpit of Lindbergh's plane was behind the large fuel tank. To see ahead, Lindbergh had to use a periscope.

Across the Oceans

Charles Lindbergh made history in 1927.
He flew a monoplane across the Atlantic
from New York, USA, to Paris, France.
No one before had ever flown so far alone.
His plane was called the *Spirit of St Louis*.

⭐ **Fact File**

A year after Lindbergh's flight, Charles Kingsford Smith and Charles Ulm flew their plane, the *Southern Cross*, across the Pacific Ocean.

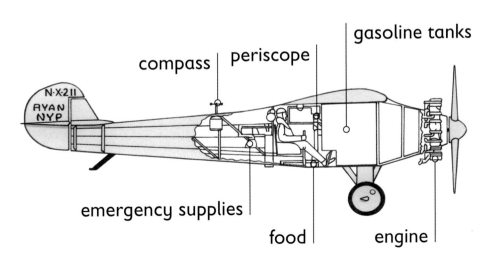

gasoline tanks

compass | periscope

N-X-2 11
RYAN
NYP

emergency supplies

food | engine

Sound Barrier

Only special airplanes can travel faster than the speed of sound. In 1947, Charles Yeager became the first to fly at supersonic speed. His plane, a Bell X–1, was shaped like a very large bullet.

Fact File

Bullets travel faster than the speed of sound. When a rifle is fired, the sharp bang you hear is a small sonic boom.

Airplanes create air waves, which spread out like ripples in a pond. When an airplane moves faster than the speed of sound, the waves hit the ground with a loud bang, called a sonic boom.

less than the
speed of sound

traveling at the
speed of sound

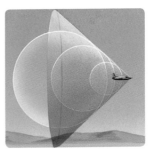

faster than the
speed of sound

At an Airport

Large, fast jet planes now take people all over the world. Each trip begins and ends at an airport, which is like a tiny city. Hundreds of airplanes take off and land there every day.

Controlling the Air

Air traffic controllers at airports keep in contact with airplane pilots. They tell the pilots when it is safe to land and to take off.

When a large airplane lands, it must quickly be unloaded, cleaned, refueled, and reloaded with food, baggage, and passengers. Then it is ready for its next journey.

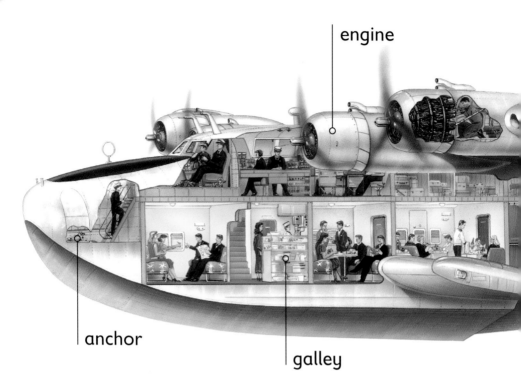

engine

anchor

galley

Seaplanes

Seaplanes take off and land on water.
Instead of wheels, they have floats or hulls
like those on ships. Large flying boats once
flew people across the oceans. Most seaplanes
are now small and carry few passengers.

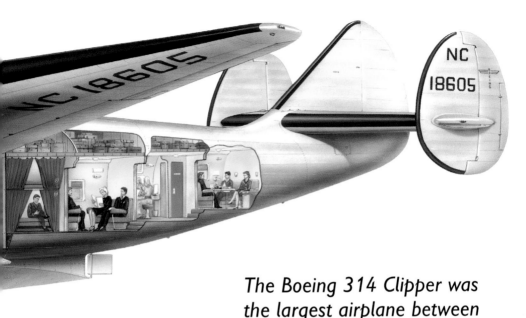

The Boeing 314 Clipper was the largest airplane between 1939 and 1946. It carried 74 passengers in great comfort.

amphibian

float plane

flying boat

Fact File

An amphibian is an airplane that can land on land or on water. It has a hull like a ship's, but also has wheels like those of other airplanes.

Helicopters

Helicopters can go straight up and down. They can also hover, and fly forward, backward, and sideways. They can get to places that airplanes cannot reach.

Fact File

Helicopters are often used in wars, to move troops quickly from one part of a battlefield to another.

Helicopters are able to rescue people who are in places that are hard to reach. This helicopter hovers as it rescues a man after an accident far out at sea.

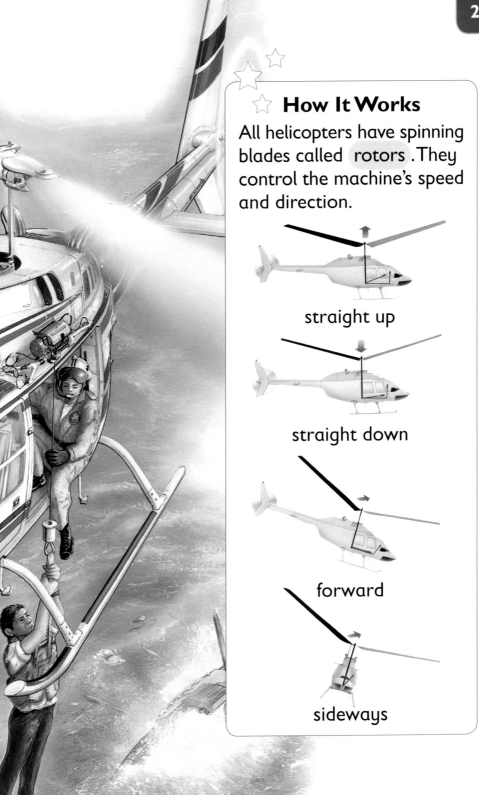

How It Works

All helicopters have spinning blades called rotors. They control the machine's speed and direction.

straight up

straight down

forward

sideways

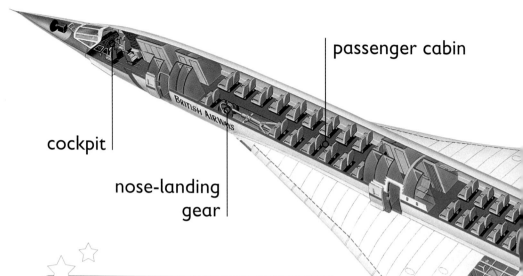

passenger cabin

cockpit

nose-landing gear

Fact File

In July 2000, a Concorde airliner crashed near Paris, France, soon after taking off. More than 100 people died in this accident.

Concorde

In 1976, Concorde, a supersonic airliner, began flying between Europe and the USA. It was twice as fast as any other passenger plane. In 2003, this airplane flew for the last time.

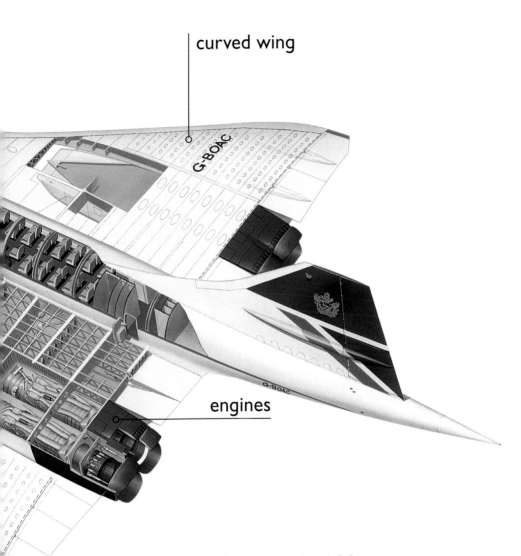

curved wing

engines

Concorde could carry only 100 passengers, and because of its loud sonic boom, it could not fly over some cities. This meant Concorde cost too much to operate. That is why no supersonic passenger airplane now flies.

Military Aircraft

Airplanes have been important in the wars of the last century. Military aircraft fight each other in the air. They drop deadly bombs on enemy positions. Most of them can now fly at supersonic speeds.

Wing Shapes

Airplane designers are always inventing new wing shapes that will help supersonic aircraft to fly faster.

delta wing

swept-back wing

swing-wing

short, thin wing

swept-forward wing

Fact File

Modern military planes have computers on board. Because of this, pilots often do not need to see targets that they want to hit.

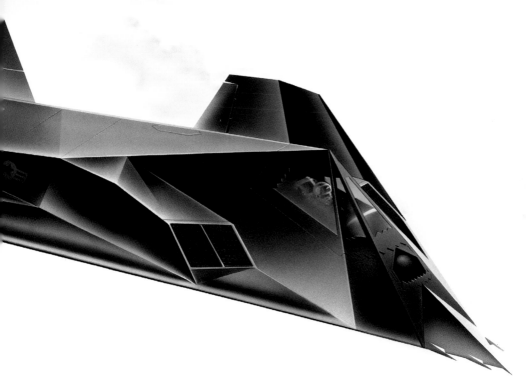

This fighter aircraft has a very unusual shape. Instead of having a rounded shape, it has thin, pointed surfaces. This makes the aircraft hard to see on radar *screens.*

Airports at Sea

Aircraft carriers are large and important warships. They carry warplanes close to the targets they are to strike. Planes take off from and land on these huge vessels' decks.

Fact File

Some aircraft carriers carry more than 80 aircraft. Most of the planes are stored in hangars below deck.

A catapault *in the deck launches the plane into the air at a speed of about 200 miles (322 km) per hour.*

Quiz

Can you unscramble the words and match them with the right pictures?

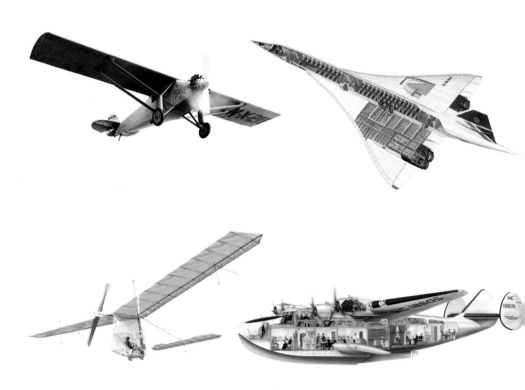

SLEEPANA

COCONERD

SMEAORGS DROONC

PLONAMENO

Glossary

aviators: people who fly airplanes or flying machines

catapault: a machine in the deck of an aircraft carrier that launches airplanes

cockpit: the section at the front of an airplane where the pilot or crew sits

gasoline: fuel that is used in motor vehicle engines

hover: to stay still in the air in the one place

muslin: a cotton cloth used to make sheets and clothing

periscope: a tube with mirrors in it that allows a person to see forward past something high

propellers: blades that spin around very quickly and pull or push airplanes through the air

radar: a system that uses radio waves to show the position and speed of objects, such as airplanes

rip cord: a rope that is pulled to release heated air or gas from inside a balloon

rotors: blades that spin around quickly and control the movement and speed of helicopters

rudders: plates at the back of ships or aircraft that control direction when moved

sonic boom: the loud noise an object makes when it travels faster than the speed of sound

supersonic: faster than the speed of sound

Index